# CHE GUEVARA

Essential Lives

# CHE GUEVARA

## POLITICAL ACTIVIST & REVOLUTIONARY

by Valerie Bodden

Content Consultant:
Michael L. Conniff, Director, Global Studies, San José State University
Anne Fountain, World Languages and Literatures, San José State University

**ABDO**
Publishing Company

# CREDITS

Published by ABDO Publishing Company, 8000 West 78th Street, Edina, Minnesota 55439. Copyright © 2011 by Abdo Consulting Group, Inc. International copyrights reserved in all countries. No part of this book may be reproduced in any form without written permission from the publisher. The Essential Library™ is a trademark and logo of ABDO Publishing Company.

Printed in the United States of America,
North Mankato, Minnesota
112010
012011

 THIS BOOK CONTAINS AT LEAST 10% RECYCLED MATERIALS.

Editor: Karen L. Kenney
Copy Editor: Paula Lewis
Interior Design and Production: Kazuko Collins
Cover Design: Kazuko Collins

**Library of Congress Cataloging-in-Publication Data**
Bodden, Valerie.
  Che Guevara : political activist and revolutionary / by Valerie Bodden.
     p. cm. — (Essential lives)
  Includes bibliographical references and index.
  ISBN 978-1-61714-780-7
  1.  Guevara, Ernesto, 1928-1967—Juvenile literature. 2.  Cuba—History—1959-1990—Juvenile literature. 3.  Latin America—History—1948-1980—Juvenile literature. 4.  Guerrillas—Latin America—Biography—Juvenile literature.  I. Title.
  F2849.22.G85B63 2011
  980.03'5092—dc22
  [B]
                              2010037883

# TABLE OF CONTENTS

| | | |
|---|---|---|
| Chapter 1 | Triumph in Cuba | 6 |
| Chapter 2 | An Argentine Youth | 14 |
| Chapter 3 | College Life | 24 |
| Chapter 4 | The Motorcycle Diaries | 32 |
| Chapter 5 | Becoming Che | 42 |
| Chapter 6 | The Revolutionary | 52 |
| Chapter 7 | A Citizen of Cuba | 64 |
| Chapter 8 | Failure in Africa | 74 |
| Chapter 9 | Ultimate Defeat | 84 |
| Timeline | | 96 |
| Essential Facts | | 100 |
| Glossary | | 102 |
| Additional Resources | | 104 |
| Source Notes | | 106 |
| Index | | 110 |
| About the Author | | 112 |

*Guevara,* center, *led rebel troops at the Battle of Santa Clara.*

# Triumph in Cuba

In late December 1958, Comandante Ernesto Che Guevara and his troops were exhausted. They had just spent four months marching more than 370 miles (595 km) across Cuba. The men were part of a revolutionary army

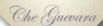

fighting under Fidel Castro to overthrow Cuba's dictator, Fulgencio Batista. Along the way, the troops had battled the Cuban army, taking control of city after city. Now, they were about to enter the city of Santa Clara. With a population of 150,000, it was Cuba's fourth-largest city. It was also one of the few remaining strongholds of the Cuban army, which had 3,500 soldiers stationed in and around the city. In comparison, Guevara had 300 guerrilla fighters. He expected the battle to be long—maybe several weeks or a month—and hard.

**Guerilla Warfare**

After World War II (1939–1945), a number of guerrilla wars were fought. Guerrillas would often capture territory and strike enemies in surprise raids. While guerrilla wars often failed, there were also some successes. In China, Mao Zedong led a Communist takeover of the government in 1949. In North Vietnam, guerrillas known as Vietminh helped a Communist government gain power.

On December 28, Guevara set up a temporary command post at Santa Clara University, which was just outside the city. From there, the revolutionary army began the five-mile (8-km) march into the city. The men walked in the ditches along the road, while Guevara rode in a jeep at the middle of the column. As they approached the city, the troops took over a radio station where Guevara broadcasted an appeal to Santa Clara's citizens to assist the rebels.

While the rebel troops marched on, planes began bombing the outskirts of the city. They were trying to hit the rebels, which caused citizens to flee to their homes. Soldiers stationed in the city also opened fire, killing five of Guevara's men in a tank attack. When the Cuban army tried to send reinforcements into Santa Clara, rebel troops blocked the highways and stopped them.

That night, with the Cuban soldiers in their barracks, the residents of Santa Clara built

### The Story of an Island

Located 90 miles (145 km) south of Key West, Florida, Cuba is a long, narrow island surrounded by the Caribbean Sea, the Atlantic Ocean, and the Gulf of Mexico. From east to west, the island stretches 777 miles (1,250 km). At its narrowest point, only 19 miles (31 km) separate its northern and southern coasts. In other areas, the island widens to 119 miles (192 km).

Christopher Columbus was the first European to land in Cuba. He claimed it for Spain in 1492. Over the following centuries, the island was settled by Spaniards. They wiped out the native populations and brought African slaves to labor on sugar plantations. Cuba remained a Spanish colony until 1898. At that time, the United States took control of the island after winning the Spanish-American War. Four years later, Cuba became an independent country.

Cuba still relied on the United States to purchase its sugar, though. During the first half of the twentieth century, many Americans vacationed in Cuba. The tourists enjoyed the island's beaches, resorts, and nightlife. The Cuban capital of Havana thrived during this time. At the time of the Cuban Revolution, Cubans enjoyed a high standard of living. In the countryside, however, the campesinos, or peasants, struggled. They were among the poorest in Latin America.

barricades to stop the army tanks. At the same time, Guevara stationed his men throughout the city. He concentrated his forces near an armored train filled with weapons, ammunition, and communications equipment intended for the Cuban army. He also ordered that a section of the railroad track be pulled up.

The next morning, the rebels began their attack against the army garrisons. As the rebels fought in the streets as well as in homes, the civilians of Santa Clara often helped them. They made Molotov cocktails, which are bombs made from glass bottles filled with gasoline. They also offered the rebels food and shelter. The army fired on the rebels and their civilian supporters from tanks and airplanes, leaving many dead and wounded.

Despite the casualties, the rebels were able to take some of the army's garrisons. The soldiers fled to the armored train in an attempt to escape the city. As the train's 22 cars built up speed, they came

**Fiercely Loyal Fighters**

Although Guevara was often harsh with his fighters, he inspired in them a fierce loyalty. While visiting wounded soldiers during the battle of Santa Clara, he met a dying man. Earlier, Guevara had disciplined him for falling asleep during battle. The man had said that his weapon was taken away because he had fired it accidentally. Guevara then told him to go to the front lines empty-handed and get a weapon from there. The man had done so. And, as Guevara reported proudly, "It seemed to me that he was pleased to have proved his courage. Such was our Rebel Army."[1]

**Guevara's Photo**

The fame Guevara gained during the Cuban Revolution lasted well after his death. Only a year after his entry into Havana, Cuban photographer Alberto Korda snapped a picture of the revolutionary wearing a beret over his long, curly hair and looking off into the distance. "There was something about his eyes, a kind of mystery,"[3] Korda later said of the photo. Today, more than 40 years after Guevara's death, the photo still appears on posters, key chains, and T-shirts.

to the section of track the rebels had removed the previous day. The train's engine and its first three cars hurtled off the track and overturned. The rebels opened fire on the cars that remained standing. Guevara described what happened next:

> *Harassed by our men who, from nearby train carriages and other close-range positions, were hurling bottles of flaming gasoline, the train—thanks to its armor-plate—became a veritable oven for its soldiers. After several hours, the entire crew surrendered . . .* [2]

The surrender of the armored train provided a major boost to the poorly armed rebels. They now had access to the Cuban army's weapons and ammunition on the train. For the next two days, the fighting continued. One after another, the army's strongholds fell to the rebels. On New Year's Day, word came that Batista had fled the country and the last army garrisons in Santa Clara had surrendered. Only six rebel soldiers had been killed; the Cuban army had nearly 300 casualties.

*An iconic image of Guevara, left, was taken by photographer Alberto Díaz Gutiérrez, center, known as Alberto Korda.*

## INTRODUCTION TO THE WORLD

The next morning, Guevara and another comandante in the revolutionary army, Camilo Cienfuegos, set out for Cuba's capital of Havana. When the men arrived—discreetly and with little fanfare—Guevara took over La Cabaña military base, as he had been ordered to by Castro. On January 7, 1959, Guevara left the city to meet Castro, who was making a slow victory march across the country. The

**A Prolific Writer**

During his lifetime, Guevara was a prolific writer. He wrote essays, articles, and books based on his travels, experiences, and theories. Some of his works were published during his life and others after his death. Among those that have been translated into English are:

• *The Motorcycle Diaries: Notes on a Latin American Journey*
• *Back on the Road: A Journey to Latin America*
• *Reminiscences of the Cuban Revolutionary War*
• *Guerrilla Warfare*
• *The African Dream: The Diaries of the Revolutionary War in the Congo*
• *The Bolivian Diary of Ernesto Che Guevara*

men entered the city together on top of a captured tank. Thousands of people lined the streets to welcome them, cheering wildly and waving flags.

Soon, pictures of the young revolutionaries' triumphant entry into Havana appeared in newspapers around the world. As Guevara wrote, "Today all eyes—those of the powerful oppressors and those of the hopeful— are fixed on us."[4]

Over the years, those eyes would continue to be fixed on Guevara as he helped steer Cuba toward communism. Until his death in 1967, he also provided Cuban support to Communist revolutions springing up across Latin America and Africa. Eventually, he disappeared from public view to participate directly in revolutions in the Congo and in Bolivia. Although both revolutions would fail—and the one in Bolivia would cost him his life—Che Guevara's legend as a tireless revolutionary would endure.

*Crowds celebrated in the streets as Castro and
the rebel army entered Havana, Cuba.*

## Chapter 2

*In 1934, Ernesto was a young child living in Argentina.*

# An Argentine Youth

The man who would one day help lead the Cuban Revolution began life far from that island. Ernesto Guevara de la Serna was the first of five children born to Ernesto Guevara Lynch and Celia de la Serna. He was

born in Rosario, Argentina, and was nicknamed "Ernestito." According to most accounts (and his birth certificate), his birth date was June 14, 1928. Biographer Jon Lee Anderson asserts the young Ernesto was actually born a month earlier on May 14, 1928. This was something Celia later confessed to a friend. She and her husband lied about the birth date, she said, because she had become pregnant before they were married. So, they had Ernesto's birth certificate falsified. Then they waited a month to announce his arrival to their families.

Ernesto's parents had traveled south to Rosario to find a comfortable hospital for the birth of their child. They actually lived nearly 1,200 miles (1,930 km) to the north in Misiones, on Argentina's border with Brazil and Paraguay. The family's plantation was on 500 acres (200 ha) of jungle along the Paraná River. Guevara Lynch farmed yerba maté. It is an evergreen shrub used to make a tea like drink popular in Argentina.

## Asthma Attacks

In late 1929, Ernesto's family again traveled south. This time, they went to Argentina's capital, Buenos Aires, where Celia gave birth to her second child. They named their daughter Celia and remained in the city after her birth. They spent the summer days at the beach. Even after winter set in, Celia continued to take young Ernesto swimming. On May 2, 1930, after swimming in cold and windy weather, her son suffered his first asthma attack.

After young Ernesto's first experience with asthma, his condition grew worse. He suffered attacks almost daily. Many nights, his father sat on Ernesto's bed. He held the boy upright against his chest to ease Ernesto's

**Land of Contrasts**

Argentina is the second-largest country in South America. It covers more than 1 million square miles (2.6 million sq km) of varying landscapes. The high, snow-capped Andes Mountains line most of the country's western border with Chile. In the northwest, between the Andes and the Paraná River, lies a hot, dry lowland known as the Gran Chaco. The northeast holds lush forests and hilly grass-lands. The flat grasslands of the Dry Pampa and the Humid Pampa cover the central part of the country. To the south, cold, windblown plateaus characterize Patagonia. In the far east, Argentina's coastline extends along 2,900 miles (4,700 km) of the Atlantic Ocean. Unlike most of South America, Argentina has a largely temperate climate. It has moderate rainfall and temperatures in most of the country.

Argentina's land contains valuable minerals, including some silver. The country was named after *argentum*, which is Latin for "silver." In the mid-nineteenth century, farmers fenced much of the fertile pampas. This allowed for increased cattle and wheat production. Argen-tina became the wealthiest nation in Latin America—and one of the wealthiest in the world—for a time. The majority of Argentina's people are of European origin, largely from Spain and Italy.

breathing. The family could not return to Misiones, where the damp climate would have aggravated the illness. When Ernesto did not improve in Buenos Aires, a doctor recommended they leave the capital.

## A Healthier Climate

From Buenos Aires, Ernesto's family moved to the small resort town of Alta Gracia located in the foothills of the Sierra Chica, a mountain range near the city of Córdoba. The family lived on money Celia had inherited from her parents. They struggled to maintain their lavish lifestyle and pay the rent. Alta Gracia's dry climate and high altitude made the city popular with vacationers and those suffering from respiratory diseases. The climate seemed to benefit Ernesto. His asthma became more manageable, although he still had frequent attacks.

When Ernesto was old enough to enter school, his numerous asthma attacks kept him from attending.

**A Strong Woman**

Most historians agree that the most important relationship in Ernesto's early life was with his mother. Celia de la Serna had strong opinions about politics and was not afraid to share them with her son. A Socialist and a feminist, she often held meetings in her home in support of Argentina's women's movement. She was among the first women in Argentina to sport short hair, wear pants, sign checks in her own name, and drive her own car.

*Ernesto's mother, Celia de la Serna, had a close bond with her son.*

Instead, his mother instructed him at home. She taught him to read and write, as well as to speak French. Their days together forged a strong bond that would last throughout his life.

When Ernesto was nearly nine years old, education authorities ordered that he begin attending school. In 1937, he entered second grade at the Escuela San Martín. Ernesto was just an average student, but he was a natural leader.

As his third-grade teacher Elba Rossi Oviedo Zelaya described,

> The children followed him around a lot in the schoolyard; he would climb up a big tree that was there, and all the kids stood around him as if he were the leader, and when he ran the others would follow behind him; it was clear that he was the boss.[1]

When Ernesto was not suffering from asthma, he was physically active. He played soccer and golf, swam, hiked, rode horses, and went target shooting. Often, these activities caused asthma attacks. Sometimes the attacks were so severe that he had to be carried home by friends. These incidents did not discourage Ernesto, though. In fact, according to his mother, they spurred him to do even more. He refused to give in to his illness.

## ANOTHER MOVE

In 1942, Ernesto began riding the bus to high school at the Colegio Nacional Deán Funes in Córdoba.

**Asthma Remedies**

Ernesto's parents were desperate to cure his asthma. They tried every remedy they could think of, including putting sandbags in his bed, changing his mattress and pillow stuffing, removing carpeting, and banning certain foods. They even once placed a live cat in his bed. But in the morning, the cat was dead. It was likely smothered when Ernesto rolled over on it. Nothing worked, though, and the asthma remained.

A year later, after his father decided to open a building firm in Córdoba, the family moved to the city. Ernesto's family was part of Argentina's social elite and lived in a two-story house. But just across the street was a large shantytown, where the poor lived in shacks of cardboard and tin.

Ernesto's family opened its doors to visitors of all social classes. According to Ernesto's friend Dolores Moyano, "Workers, mechanics, caddies, newsboys, people from all walks of life would meet to socialize with the Guevaras' upper-class friends."[2] Moyano also noted a level of freedom in the family's life:

> *Mealtimes were not fixed; one just ate when one felt hungry. You were free to ride your bicycle from the street through the living room into their backyard. In the house, one could hardly see the furniture for the books and magazines piled high everywhere.*[3]

**A Long Line of Ancestors**

Ernesto came from a long line of wealthy Argentine nobility. On his mother's side, one ancestor had been the Spanish viceroy of Peru. Another was a famous Argentine general. In addition, 12 generations of his father's family had lived in Argentina and had amassed great wealth. But by the time Ernesto Guevara Lynch was born, the family's fortune had dwindled.

Despite the family's long history in Argentina, Ernesto's paternal grandmother and grandfather were born in California. Their families had gone there in search of gold during the late 1840s.

In high school, Ernesto remained an average student. He received high marks in literature and philosophy but poor scores in music, physics, and English language classes. He also participated in team sports, including the English game of rugby, but he was often driven off the field by asthma attacks. Through willpower, an inhaler, and injections of adrenaline, Ernesto controlled the attacks. Despite his asthma, he was a fierce player who would often run at other players yelling, "Here comes El Furibundo [Furious] Serna."[4] Alberto Granado, Ernesto's friend and coach, shortened this name to "Fuser." Others called him "Chancho," meaning filthy, because he bragged that he rarely washed his clothing or himself. Still another nickname was "El Loco" (The Crazy One) Guevara. This was given to him for his reckless actions, such as walking over gorges on narrow pipelines and biking on train tracks.

**Wild Stunts**

According to many of his schoolmates, young Ernesto was a show-off who tried to gain attention with wild stunts. He drank ink and ate chalk in grade school, even after students had been warned that ink and chalk were poisonous. He hung from a railroad bridge, ventured into a dangerous mine shaft, and shot firecrackers into a neighbor's house during a party. And if he was going to be punished for his actions, he ran off into the countryside. He remained there until his parents were so worried about him that they forgot to punish him.

While in high school, Ernesto showed little interest in politics. His one political view was a dislike for the United States, which was common of the youth in Córdoba at the time. As he later wrote, "I had no social preoccupations in my adolescence and had no participation in the political or student struggles in Argentina."[5]

*Even as a young man, Ernesto was a natural leader whose schoolmates would follow him around the schoolyard.*

*Juan Perón was sworn in as the twenty-ninth president of Argentina in 1946.*

# COLLEGE LIFE

After graduating from high school, Ernesto planned to study engineering in Córdoba. But in 1947, his grandmother in Buenos Aires fell ill. Ernesto joined his family there and arrived 17 days before she passed away.

After her death, Ernesto decided to study medicine at the University of Buenos Aires. He had been frustrated at being able to do little to ease his grandmother's pain as she died. He was also likely inspired to study medicine to understand more about his own asthma.

Shortly before his nineteenth birthday, Ernesto entered the university. Although he rarely attended class, he spent long hours studying to pass the exams at the end of each term. In addition to his studies, Ernesto worked as a research assistant at an allergy clinic. During this time, Ernesto's parents informally separated. His father continued living in the family home, sleeping on the couch.

In 1946, the year before Ernesto entered medical school, Argentina had undergone a major shift as Juan Perón became president. During Ernesto's years at the university, Perón's regime became notorious for eliminating constitutional liberties

**A Favored Son**

In 1946, Ernesto's mother, Celia, was diagnosed with breast cancer. Some in the family believed her illness was one factor in Ernesto's decision to pursue medicine. After Celia's diagnosis, she and Ernesto grew even closer. Family friends often noticed that she seemed to favor her eldest son over her other children. According to relatives, Celia's favoritism was especially hard on Ernesto's younger brother Roberto. Though Roberto excelled at rugby, he was often eclipsed by Ernesto. While not a skilled player, Ernesto had overcome asthma to participate in the sport.

## Odd Jobs

In addition to working at an allergy clinic while attending medical school, Ernesto took on a number of other odd jobs. For a short time, he founded and edited a rugby magazine called *Tackle,* but it folded after 11 issues. He also worked to develop a roach-killing insecticide but stopped when he and his workers began to get sick. Afterward, he bought a large supply of shoes cheaply and attempted to resell them. He purchased the shoes without seeing them, however, and discovered that they were mismatched leftovers. After selling all of the matching pairs he could find, Ernesto kept and wore the mismatched shoes himself.

and throwing political opponents in jail. While other students protested Perón, Ernesto spoke little of his country's president. He seemed neither to strongly support nor oppose him. Ernesto also did not become involved in student organizations. Although he once joined a friend at a meeting of the Communist Youth, he walked out before the meeting was over.

## On the Road

On weekends and during school breaks, Ernesto often hitchhiked back to Córdoba with his friend Carlitos Figueroa. The 400-mile (645-km) journey would have taken ten hours by car. But often, it took them three days riding on the backs of trucks, and they usually had to unload the trucks to pay their way.

In January 1950, Ernesto decided to take more than a weekend jaunt. He left for a solo six-week tour of northern Argentina on a bicycle fitted with a small motor. He brought along two changes of

On a bicycle fitted with a motor, Ernesto toured
Argentina for six weeks in 1950.

clothing, a thermos, and some food. After spending
several days in Córdoba, Ernesto biked to the town
of San Francisco del Chañar. He visited his old
friend Alberto Granado, who worked at a hospital
for lepers there. Ernesto then continued north to
Argentina's border with Chile and Bolivia. Along

the way, he often found free shelter in hospitals and police stations. Traveling through Argentina's indigenous communities, he saw their poverty for the first time.

During the course of his travels, Ernesto came to believe that "the soul of a people is reflected in the sick in the hospitals, the men in custody at police stations or the anxious pedestrian with whom one enters into conversation."[1] In mid–February, Ernesto returned to Buenos Aires to begin his fourth year of medical school, having traveled more than 2,485 miles (4,000 km).

## Biking for Nothing?

During his trip to northern Argentina, Ernesto stopped to inflate a tire and met a tramp living in a culvert. The man had recently taken part in Argentina's cotton harvest. After doing nothing for a time, he was planning to travel south to look for work harvesting grapes. When the man realized that Ernesto was traveling with no greater purpose than recreation, he grabbed his head, saying, "Mamma mia, all that effort for nothing?"[2] Ernesto had no response.

Later, however, exulting in the beauty of northern Argentina's tropical forest and lamenting the fact that even here he could not escape the sounds of civilization, he reflected on what he had learned about himself during the trip:

*I then realized that something has matured in me, something that had been growing inside me for some time while surrounded by the din of cities: and it is a hatred of urban civilization; the vulgar image of people moving as madmen to the tune of that enormous noise, which to me seems the hated antithesis [opposite] of peace . . . in which the almost silent rustling of leaves is like melodious background music.[3]*

## First Love

Shortly after returning from his trip, 22-year-old Ernesto fell in love with María del Carmen Ferreyra, known as "Chichina" to her friends. Although he had known Chichina from Córdoba, they met again at a wedding in October 1950. As Chichina, who was 16 at the time, described,

> *I saw him . . . and I was thunderstruck. He had an impact on me, a tremendous impact, this man was coming down the stairs and then we started talking and we spent the whole night talking about books.*[4]

Chichina was the daughter of one of the wealthiest families in Córdoba. Her family owned a mansion in the city and an elegant summer estate called Malagueño. As Ernesto's friend (and Chichina's cousin) Dolores Moyano pointed out, "In many ways, Malagueño exemplified everything Ernesto despised. Yet, unpredictable as always, Ernesto had fallen madly in love with the princess of this little empire . . ."[5]

**Provoking Comments**

Ernesto seemed to take special delight in exasperating his girlfriend Chichina's family. One night, several of her family members were praising British Prime Minister Winston Churchill. Ernesto then spoke poorly of the politician. After Chichina's father left the room in disgust, Ernesto "merely smiled like a naughty child and began eating a lemon in bites, peel and all," according to a friend who was with him.[6]

Although he was in love with Chichina, Ernesto did not try to fit in with her family. He continued to care little about his appearance. He wore dirty shirts, scuffed-up shoes, and baggy pants that sometimes were held up with a piece of clothesline. Often, his appearance brought the conversation at a party to a stop. Ernesto enjoyed the sensation he created, though. "Mysteriously, instead of his being embarrassed by all of us, it always worked the other way around," Moyano said.[7]

Soon, Ernesto was convinced that he and Chichina should get married, but her parents did not agree. The young couple continued to see each other secretly, but Chichina did not say yes to his proposal.

Although Ernesto's relationship with Chichina was still new, he left home during a break from school in February 1951. Sailing aboard a petroleum company ship, he worked as a nurse. He traveled to locations such as Brazil, Guyana, and Venezuela. Ernesto did not enjoy life as a sailor, though. He wanted to spend less time at sea and more time exploring on land. ⌒

In a scene from the film The Motorcycle Diaries, Ernesto is portrayed dancing with his girlfriend, Chichina Ferreyra.

In the film The Motorcycle Diaries, *Alberto Granado's character,* left, is shown with *Ernesto's character* on their trip.

# THE MOTORCYCLE DIARIES

After completing his stint as a sailor, Ernesto returned to Buenos Aires in June 1951. He was entering his fifth year of medical school. By October, however, he had agreed to embark on a tour of South America with his friend,

Alberto Granado. He and Alberto planned to make the trip on Alberto's motorcycle, nicknamed *La Poderosa II.* That name is Spanish for "The Powerful One II." In early January 1952, the two friends loaded the motorcycle with a grill, a tent, and extra clothes and set out on their trip.

Their first stop was Miramar, which is a beach resort on Argentina's coast. Ernesto said good-bye to Chichina and tried to convince her to wait for him. He gave her a puppy that he named Come-Back. It was a symbol of his intention to return to her.

On January 14, Ernesto and Alberto left Miramar and headed south for Argentina's Dry Pampa, which neither had seen before. By early February, they reached Argentina's Lake District near the border of Chile at the edge of the Andes Mountains. They hiked

**Free Food**

With their meager funds, Ernesto and Alberto often had to beg for food. Soon, they worked out a routine to get a free meal. First, one of the young men would mention that it was the first anniversary of the day they had begun their journey. Alberto would then lament that they could not celebrate the occasion since they had no money. Usually, the person to whom they were talking would offer to buy them a drink, which they would accept. When the person offered them another, however, Ernesto would refuse. He confessed with embarrassment that in Argentina people traditionally drink while eating. Soon, they would have their meal.

around the area's breathtaking lakes and climbed a peak—and almost fell off. Since they were already running low on money, they frequently asked roadside families for food and shelter. At other times, they slept in their tent.

While they were in the area, Ernesto received a letter from Chichina breaking off their relationship. He recorded in his journal how he felt:

*I read and reread the incredible letter. Just like that, all my dreams of home, bound up with those eyes that saw me off in Miramar, came crashing down for what seemed like no reason.* [1]

---

### An Eye-Opening Experience

During Ernesto's tour of South America, he came in contact with the continent's poorest people. In Chile, he was asked to help an elderly servant woman who was dying. He did his best to make her more comfortable and was angered by her family's obvious lack of care. On another occasion, he met a poor miner. The man had been jailed for taking part in a labor strike and was now traveling with his wife in search of work in the country's dangerous sulfur mines. After giving the couple a blanket to protect them against the cold night air of the desert mountains, Ernesto realized that "it was one of the coldest times in my life, but also one which made me feel a little more brotherly toward this strange, for me at least, human species."[2]

Despite an emerging concern for the poor, Ernesto took part in injustices at times. In one situation in Peru, he denied to a police officer that another officer, who was drunk, had shot a hole in the wall of a bar owned by an Indian woman. This was untrue. Ernesto had seen the officer do so. Determined not to anger the drunken officer—who had paid for their food—Alberto and Ernesto took the blame. They said they had lit off a firecracker and then they fled.

## SEEING SOUTH AMERICA

Despite his disappointment, Ernesto went forward with his journey. He and Alberto arrived in Chile on February 13 aboard a leaky boat on which they worked the bilge pumps. They continued travelling by motorcycle. It soon gave out, though, and they left it behind in the Chilean capital of Santiago. As Alberto later noted, losing the motorcycle turned out to be for the best:

> There is no doubt that the trip would not have been as useful and beneficial as it was, as a personal experience, if the motorcycle had held out. . . . This gave us a chance to become familiar with the people.[3]

Without the motorcycle, the travelers continued by hitchhiking and, on one occasion, by stowing away on a ship. They earned money to pay their way by taking odd jobs as dishwashers, salesmen, and even physicians (by claiming to be doctors with an expertise in leprosy). When they could not find work, they resorted to begging for food.

From Chile, Ernesto and Alberto passed into Peru. They hitched rides aboard trucks carrying people and animals through the Andes. The two were often invited to ride in the cabs of the trucks while

**The Ruins of
Machu Picchu**

Although he fell in love
with the ruins of Machu
Picchu, Ernesto was
annoyed by the presence
of North American tour-
ists. He did not believe
the tourists belonged
there. In an article later
published in Panama, he
wrote of the discovery
of the city by American
Hiram Bingham:

"Here comes the sad
part. All the ruins were
cleared of overgrowth,
perfectly studied and
described and . . . totally
robbed of every object
that fell into the hands
of the researchers. . . .
Where can one go to
admire or study the trea-
sures of the indigenous
city? The answer is obvi-
ous: in the museums of
North America."[5]

indigenous travelers were forced to
ride in the open backs. As they passed
through native villages, Ernesto was
moved by the plight of the people
living there:

> These people who watch us walk through
> the streets of the town are a defeated race.
> . . . Some give the impression they go on
> living only because it's a habit they cannot
> shake.[4]

High in the Andes, the two
young men visited the ancient Incan
city of Machu Picchu. Ernesto was
enchanted by the ruins. From there,
the men traveled to the Peruvian
capital of Lima and stayed there for
three weeks before moving on to the
country's Amazon region. In the
jungle, Ernesto's asthma flared up,
and he could not continue traveling
for several days. On June 8, the two
young men arrived at the San Pablo
leprosarium, an isolated village of
600 lepers. For two weeks, Ernesto

*On his travels, Ernesto visited many countries throughout South America and also stopped in Miami, Florida, for a short stay.*

and Alberto worked with San Pablo's doctors, played soccer with the patients, and enjoyed excursions through the rain forest. As they prepared to leave, the lepers they had befriended presented them with a raft. The two young men used it to set out down the Amazon River.

After rafting for three days, they caught a ride aboard a native boat to travel upriver to the Colombian port of Leticia. There, they worked as soccer coaches before flying to Colombia's capital, Bogotá. They arrived in Bogotá during the height of a civil war known as La Violencia. Ernesto noted the city's tense conditions in a letter to his mother:

> *There is more repression of individual freedom here than in any country we've been to, the police patrol the streets carrying rifles. . . . We're getting out of here as soon as we can.*[6]

The police gave Ernesto and Alberto some trouble when they found that Ernesto had a knife. It had been given to him by his brother as a going-away present. The travelers were soon released, however, and quickly left Bogotá and Columbia.

Ernesto and Alberto headed for Caracas, the capital of Venezuela. They arrived in mid-July. Alberto was offered a job at a leprosarium, which he decided to take. Ernesto, meanwhile, was offered a spot on a flight to Argentina with a brief stopover in the United States to deliver racehorses. He promised that once he had obtained his medical degree, he would return to Venezuela and join Alberto at the leprosarium.

On July 26, Ernesto flew to Miami, Florida. He remained in the city for a month while the plane underwent repairs. Although he despised the United States, Ernesto spent much of his time going to the beach and exploring Miami.

## Back to Argentina

On August 31, 1952, Ernesto returned to Buenos Aires. He immediately delved into studying for the 14 exams he still had to pass to receive his medical degree. He also went back to work at the allergy clinic. In his spare time, he composed the notes from his travel journal into a book. It was later published as *Notas de Viaje*, which in English means *The Motorcycle Diaries*. In the introduction

### Alberto after the Tour

After touring through South America with Ernesto, Alberto worked at a leprosarium in Venezuela for several years. He also married a Venezuelan woman. After Ernesto's victory in the Cuban Revolution, Alberto and his family moved to Cuba, where he became a professor of biochemistry at the University of Havana.

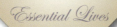

to the book, he wrote about how his journey had affected him: "I am not the person I once was. All this wandering around 'Our America with a capital A' has changed me more than I thought."[7]

On April 11, 1953, Ernesto completed his last exam. He was now Dr. Ernesto Guevara de la Serna.

*In 1953, Ernesto earned his medical degree from
the University of Buenos Aires.*

*People ran through the streets of La Paz, Bolivia,
during the country's revolution in 1952.*

# BECOMING CHE

By July 1953, only a few months after completing his last exam, Guevara was ready to leave his homeland again. This time, he planned to make his way to Venezuela to meet up with Alberto Granado as he had promised. Traveling with him was a friend from his youth, Carlos Ferrer. As Guevara left Argentina for Bolivia, he wrote in a new journal,

> My helper's name has changed. . . . But the trip is the same: two separate wills moving out through the [South] American continent, not knowing the exact aim of their quest nor in which direction lies their objective.[1]

In Bolivia, Guevara and Ferrer witnessed unrest, as a revolutionary movement had taken power only a year before. Guevara wanted to learn more about the revolution. He spent much of his time talking with the politicians involved in the reform movement. After nearly a month in Bolivia, the two travelers again set out on the road. They visited Machu Picchu and Lima, Peru, before continuing to Ecuador. Staying in Ecuador's busy port city of Guayaquil for three weeks, they lived

## Leftist Governments

A leftist government is one that believes all people should be politically, financially, and socially equal. Such governments generally support state control of a country's land and industry and favor the working class. They often attempt to redistribute the wealth and land of the rich to the poor. Both socialism and communism are examples of leftist governments.

During the mid-twentieth century, a number of leftist governments came to power around the world. They were often opposed by the United States and resented its interference, which they considered imperialist. An imperialist country is one that attempts to control another, either by forcefully taking it over or by wielding strong economic or political influence.

in a single room with four other Argentines. These men convinced Guevara to abandon his plans for Venezuela and to travel to Guatemala instead. A coup had occurred there a decade earlier and had brought to power a leftist government that supported farming and labor reforms. That government was now fighting to stay in control. Guevara left Ecuador on October 31 and spent the next two months traveling toward Guatemala. Along the way, he spent time in Costa Rica, Panama, and Nicaragua.

### Fidel Castro

Fidel Castro was born in 1926 to a relatively wealthy Cuban family. A natural leader, he quickly became involved in student politics at the University of Havana, where he studied law. Although he did not identify himself as a Communist at the time, he despised imperialism. He blamed the United States and its United Fruit Company for making Cuba dependent on sugar exports and an unfair land-ownership system. This system granted huge estates to a few privileged Cubans, while leaving plantation workers in poverty. In 1947, he tried to join an expedition to overthrow the government of the neighboring Dominican Republic, but the mission was never carried out.

In 1952, Castro attempted to run for a seat in Cuba's House of Representatives. Dictator Fulgencio Batista had just come to power in a military coup and cancelled the elections. Unable to work within the government, Castro tried to overthrow it. On July 26, 1953, he led a group of young revolutionaries in an attack on the Moncada army barracks in eastern Cuba, but he was quickly defeated. Eight rebels were killed in the fighting and 69 were executed or tortured to death. Others, including Castro, were imprisoned. Although sentenced to 15 years, he was freed in May 1955. He then immediately went to Mexico and began planning another attempt at a revolution.

## Political Awakening

Guevara arrived in Guatemala City in late December 1953. Shortly after, he met Hilda Gadea—a revolutionary exile from Peru. Although the two would soon begin a relationship, Gadea later wrote of their first meeting: "Guevara made a negative impression on me. He seemed too superficial to be an intelligent man, egotistical and conceited."[2]

With Gadea's help, Guevara was introduced to government leaders. Gadea also connected Guevara with a group of Cuban exiles who had fled their country after attempting to overthrow the government of Fulgencio Batista on July 26, 1953. Guevara quickly developed a friendship with the Cubans and spent hours talking with them about the 26th of July Movement and its leader, Fidel Castro. As Guevara spoke with the Cubans, he frequently used the word *che*. This is an Argentine expression meaning "hey you." Soon, the Cubans called him "Che," a nickname that would last throughout his adult life.

While in Guatemala, Guevara also read a number of political works. Many were by Communist authors such as Karl Marx, Friedrich Engels, and Vladimir

*Guevara read works by Communist authors, including Vladimir Lenin, while developing his political ideology.*

Lenin. Guevara began to develop a political ideology. He identified with Marxism, which advocates the formation of Communist states through violent revolution.

In June 1954, a group of American mercenaries and Guatemalan exiles, directed by the US Central Intelligence Agency (CIA), invaded the country and

bombed Guatemala City. Guevara believed that the government of Guatemala should provide the people with weapons to fight the invasion. But he was sorely disappointed when President Jacobo Arbenz resigned with little resistance. The entire incident increased his hostility toward the United States, which had been protecting the interests of the American-owned United Fruit Company in Guatemala.

Under Guatemala's new government that was backed by the United States, people suspected of Communist leanings were arrested. Guevara took refuge at the Argentine embassy. He remained there for a month before embarking on a new journey for yet another country— Mexico.

## JOINING THE REVOLUTION

By mid-September 1954, Guevara reached Mexico City. Soon after

**Communist Ideologies**

In 1848, the German philosophers Karl Marx and Friedrich Engels published *Manifesto of the Communist Party*, which became the basis for modern communism. In it, they recounted the history of the struggle between the working class and the ruling class. They also laid out their ideal of a classless society in which private property was abolished and everyone would work for the common good. In order to achieve such an ideal, Marx and Engels believed revolution was necessary. They concluded their book with a call to arms: "Working men of all countries, unite!"[3] Later Communists, such as Russian Vladimir Lenin, believed that the revolution would be sparked not by the working class but by a Communist party made up of middle-class intellectuals who would direct the uneducated masses.

arriving, he was reunited with Gadea. She had been jailed briefly after the revolution in Guatemala before being sent to Mexico. The two continued the relationship they had begun in Guatemala.

For a time, Guevara survived by taking pictures of tourists in the Mexican capital. He was then offered a job in the allergy department of the city's General Hospital. Although his new position paid little, it changed the course of Guevara's life. During his time at the hospital, he was reunited with Ñico López, one of the Cuban exiles he had grown close to in Guatemala. During the summer of 1955, López took Guevara to meet Raúl Castro. He then introduced the Argentine to his brother, Fidel. Fidel Castro was not a Communist and in fact pledged to restore democracy and justice to Cuba. Despite this, Guevara was impressed by the revolutionary leader and recorded meeting Fidel Castro in his journal:

### Political Connections

While looking for a job as a doctor in Guatemala, Guevara learned that it would be almost impossible to obtain one without the right political connections. At one point, he was offered a position on the condition that he join the Guatemalan Communist Party. Although he had already begun to identify with the ideas of communism, Guevara angrily refused. He said that he would join the party when he was ready to and not because he had been coerced.

*A political event was that I met Fidel Castro, the Cuban revolutionary. He is a young, intelligent guy, very sure of himself and extraordinarily audacious [bold]; I think we hit it off well.*[4]

Castro spoke at length of his plans to overthrow Batista. Having taken over the Cuban government in a military coup, Batista now ruled as a ruthless dictator. He controlled Cuba's university, its press, and even its congress. He also funneled money from the government into his own pocket. Soon, Guevara agreed to join the Cubans in a new attempt to overthrow the corrupt dictator.

In early August 1955, Gadea learned that she was pregnant. Shortly afterward, on August 18, she and Guevara married. Their daughter, Hilda (whom they called Hildita), was born on February 15, 1956.

## Training for Revolution

Around the time of Hildita's birth, Guevara and the Cubans began physical training for the revolution they planned to mount. They walked around Mexico City and hiked the hills that surround the capital. They also hiked up the 17,930-foot (5,465-m) volcano Popocatépetl.

In May 1956, the aspiring guerrilla fighters moved to a training camp just outside the city. Guevara was named chief of personnel at the camp. He and the group's trainer, Alberto Bayo, led the men on long endurance marches, often at night, with little food or water. The men also participated in simulated combat, learned to make Molotov cocktails, and studied guerrilla strategy. By the end of the training period, Bayo told Castro that Guevara was "beyond all doubt the best man."[5]

In late June, Mexican authorities learned of the operation. They arrested Guevara, Castro, and the other Cuban guerrillas. A month later, most of the revolutionaries were freed, but Guevara remained in jail on charges of overstaying his visa. Finally, in mid-August, he too was released. For the next three months, Guevara and the Cubans laid low in Mexico while completing their preparations.

### Insubordination at Camp

As one of the leaders of the training camp in Mexico, Guevara had to ensure discipline among his men. When Calixto Morales, a recruit, refused to walk any farther during a training march, Guevara called for a court martial. After the trial, Castro felt that Morales should be executed. That way, the "contagious disease" of his insubordination would not spread to the other men.[6] Guevara, however, argued that Morales should be allowed to live. Castro later pardoned the young man. According to some witnesses, at least one man who was believed to be a spy was executed during the training period.

In 1957, Fidel Castro was the leader of the Cuban Revolution.

*General Fulgencio Batista, with arms raised, was overthrown from power by the Cuban Revolution.*

# THE REVOLUTIONARY

Early on the morning of November 25, 1956, Guevara, Castro, and 80 other men made their way onto the *Granma*, a small, overloaded yacht. They sailed out of the Tuxpan River in Mexico toward Cuba, where they intended to start a revolution. A week later, on December 2, they reached the island but missed their intended landing site. They were forced to beach their boat on a sandbar at the edge of a mangrove swamp. Leaving many of their supplies behind, the men slogged through the swamp toward dry ground.

The landing of the *Granma* was intended to coincide with an uprising in the city of Santiago by forces from the 26th of July Movement. But the boat arrived two days later than expected, and the uprising had been carried out without Guevara's group. Afterward, Batista sent air force and navy patrols to the coast on alert for the arrival of the group from Mexico. Now, as the newly landed rebels tried to make their way to the safety of the Sierra Maestra Mountains, planes sprayed the area with gunfire.

Only three days after landing in Cuba, the rebels faced their first attack by the Cuban army, which surprised them near Alegría de Pío. The rebels scattered and became separated; several were wounded. Guevara was hit in the neck by a bullet but received only a flesh wound. Although he had been brought on the expedition as a doctor, Guevara later recorded that during this battle he had to choose between the tools he would need as a doctor and those he would need as a soldier: "At my feet were a pack full of medicines and a cartridge box; together, they were too heavy to carry. I chose the cartridge box, leaving behind the medicine pack . . ."[1]

For more than two weeks after the battle at Alegría de Pío, Guevara and a small group traveled into the Sierra Maestra. They finally met up with other survivors, including Castro. The original rebel army of 82 men had been reduced to just 22.

---

### Guevara's Reported Death

During the Cuban Revolution, reports circulated that Guevara had been killed in battle. The first were issued almost immediately after the rebels landed in Cuba in December 1956. Batista claimed that the Cuban army had been victorious in defeating the rebel army and killing its leaders, including Fidel and Raúl Castro and Guevara.

In Mexico City, Gadea learned of the report at work, but friends encouraged her to hold out hope since the news had not been confirmed. In Buenos Aires, Guevara's father went to the offices of the newspaper *La Prensa* seeking confirmation of the news, but reporters could offer none. It was not until around Christmas that the family learned from the Argentine ambassador in Cuba, who was a relative, that Guevara was not among the dead, wounded, or imprisoned rebels. On New Year's Eve, they rejoiced to receive a letter from Guevara: "Dear old folks: I am perfectly, I spent two [lives] and have five left."[2]

During the revolution's final battle at Santa Clara, it was again widely reported that Guevara had died. This time, it took only a day for the rumors to be quelled. An announcement on the rebels' radio station, Radio Rebelde, stated that he was still alive and about to achieve victory in the battle.

## First Blood

By mid-January 1957, the ranks of the rebel army had grown slightly to 32 as peasants began joining the fight. On January 16, the rebels mounted their first attack, assaulting a small military barracks in the village of La Plata. The soldiers in the barracks quickly surrendered. Guevara later wrote of what the victory achieved: "It came to everyone's attention, proving that the Rebel Army existed and was ready to fight. For us, it was the reaffirmation of the possibility of our final triumph."[3]

Shortly after La Plata, the rebel army engaged in another battle. During this battle, Guevara killed his first enemy soldier. He wrote matter-of-factly of the incident, "He had a bullet under the heart with exit on the right side, he was dead."[4] The men then spent several weeks marching through the mountains

**Fighting for Cuba**

Throughout the Cuban Revolution, a number of reporters from around the world trekked into the Sierra Maestra Mountains to interview Castro and Guevara. When Jorge Ricardo Masetti, an Argentine reporter, asked Guevara why he was fighting in Cuba, which was not his homeland, he received this response: "In the first place, I consider my fatherland to be not only Argentina, but all of [Latin] America. . . . What is more, I cannot conceive that it can be called interference to give myself personally, to give myself completely, to offer my blood for a cause I consider just and popular, to help a people liberate themselves from tyranny."[5]

*Raul Castro, left, his brother Fidel Castro, center, and Camilo Cienfuegos,
right, set up a rebel camp in the Sierra Maestra Mountains.*

while being pursued by the army, which often sent
civilians to spy on them. In mid-February, one of
those spies became the first to be executed—and
Guevara was the one to fire the shot.

In late February, Guevara suffered from a severe
asthma attack that made it difficult for him to keep

up with the other men. Castro ordered him to stay behind to await a delivery of medicine and meet up with a group of new rebel volunteers. After carrying out his mission—which brought the rebel army's total force to 70 men—Guevara rejoined Castro, and the men ranged the mountains. They avoided confrontation with the Cuban army as they trained the new men and tried to win peasant support.

### Becoming a Combatant

In May 1957, the rebel army received a large supply of new weapons. Guevara was given a Madsen automatic rifle. He proudly marked the occasion, writing, "In this way, I made my debut as a fighting guerrilla, for until then I had been the troop's doctor, knowing only occasional combat."[6] Later that month, on May 28, the rebels attacked an army garrison at El Uvero. Within hours, they had won what Guevara saw as a decisive victory, which boosted morale significantly.

Despite the rebel victory, six guerrillas had been killed, two were in critical condition, and seven more were injured. Castro assigned Guevara to remain behind to care for the wounded and move them to safety as the rest of the column marched back into

The Cuban army led its soldiers to fear Guevara by spreading propaganda about the guerrilla leader. According to one Cuban soldier who joined the rebel army after being captured, "[The army] said that he was a murderer for hire, a pathological criminal . . . a mercenary, who lent his services to international communism, that he used terrorist methods and that he [brainwashed] the women and took away their sons. . . . [It was said] any soldiers he took prisoner he tied to a tree and opened up their guts with a bayonet."[8]

the mountains. After several weeks, Guevara's group headed toward the main column, gaining new recruits along the way. When Guevara rejoined Castro's group on July 17, he was rewarded for his successful mission by receiving the higher rank of captain.

## Comandante Guevara

Only a few days after Guevara's promotion to captain, Castro promoted him again. He told Guevara to sign his rank as *comandante*, which means "commander." This was the highest rank in the rebel army, and so far, only Castro had held it. "The vanity which we all have in us made me the proudest man in the world that day," Guevara later wrote.[7] He was given a small star as a symbol of his rank.

Guevara was now the commander of his own column of the revolutionary army, and he immediately set out in search of the Cuban army. He would lead several battles in the coming months, including El Bueycito in July, El Hombrito in August, and Pino del Agua in September. Although there were some deserters, many of Guevara's men became intensely loyal to him, largely because he led by example. He lived, ate, and fought with his men without accepting any special privileges. "He was a man who liked to take the lead in combat, to set an example; he would never say, go and fight, but rather, follow me into combat," according to Harry Villegas, who fought with Guevara.[9]

By the end of October, Guevara had begun to establish a permanent base at El Hombrito, a valley in the Sierra Maestra. He had set up a hospital, a pig farm, and an armory to produce grenades and other weapons. He had also established the guerrilla newspaper *El Cubano Libre,* which is Spanish for The Free Cuban. When the base was destroyed by the enemy in early December, Guevara spent the early part of 1958 setting up a new headquarters at La Mesa. In March, he established a guerrilla training school at Minas del Frío.

### Daring Driver

In April 1958, Castro summoned Guevara to his headquarters to plan strategy. Guevara jumped behind the wheel of a jeep with one of the rebel army's new recruits, Oscar Fernández Mell, and drove along a narrow, unpaved mountain road atop steep cliffs at high speed. It was only when they got to their destination that Guevara confessed to Mell that this was the first time he had ever driven a car.

In May, the Cuban army began an offensive, bringing 10,000 troops against the 300 rebels. For the next three months, Guevara traveled back and forth between the front line and the rebels' command centers, directing operations, strengthening the front lines, and fortifying defensive positions. Although the rebels often had to draw back, they were able to pick off isolated army units and soon gained ground. By August 7, the rebels had forced the Cuban army to retreat.

## Toward Victory

After the army's retreat, Castro decided to expand the war across Cuba. He sent Guevara's column of 148 men on a march to Las Villas province in the center of the country. Along the way, they were to take out army garrisons and prevent the movement of enemy troops between the eastern and western halves of the island. Although Guevara initially planned to travel by truck, the Cuban army was able to intercept delivery

### Guevara's Companions

Although Guevara found Gadea to be a suitable companion, especially because of their shared political goals, he married her largely because she became pregnant with his child. After leaving Mexico for Cuba, Guevara sent few letters to his wife, and his diary entries from the time make no reference to her. While in Cuba, Guevara met Aleida March, the daughter of poor white farmers. Although March was anticommunist when she met Guevara, the two began a serious relationship. She later became his second wife.

*Cuban President Fulgencio Batista voted on November 3, 1958,
in an election that was rigged for his successor to win.*

of the gasoline he needed for the trip. Beginning
on August 31, he and his men marched for six
weeks. They covered more than 370 miles (595 km),
marching through swamps and across flooded rivers
in nearly constant rain. They had little food or water
and were often fired on from the air and tracked by
the army on the ground.

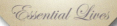

By mid-October, the men finally reached Las
Villas province. They disrupted traffic and kept most
of the population from turning out for elections
on November 3, which were rigged to give Batista's
handpicked successor the victory. After the elections,
Guevara established a base at Caballete de Casas
in the province's Escambray Mountains. He met a
young revolutionary named Aleida March and began
a romantic relationship with her. Soon, she was at
his side, even in combat.

Throughout November and December,
Guevara's column closed roads, destroyed bridges,
and disrupted railroad routes. This effectively split
the island and blocked the arrival of Cuban army
reinforcements. Throughout December, the rebels
took one town after another. During the last days of
the year, they successfully attacked Santa Clara. By
January 1959, the revolutionary army had entered
Havana and was in control of Cuba.

*Castro, Guevara, and other revolutionaries triumphantly entered Havana, Cuba, on January 1, 1959.*

*Guevara's parents visited him in Havana, Cuba, in 1959.*

# A Citizen of Cuba

After making a triumphant entry into Havana with Castro, Guevara and March settled in an officer's house at La Cabaña military base. Guevara now presided over the trials of accused spies and war criminals; many

were sentenced to be executed by firing squad.
Historians estimate that between 200 and 700
people were executed during the first months of
the new regime. Although people around the world
objected, many in Cuba supported the executions.
Batista's supporters were known to have committed
many atrocious crimes, including murder. Guevara
viewed the executions as a necessary step in removing
disloyal forces and ensuring that the revolution
would not be overthrown. Old friends, shocked
to find Guevara so hardened, asked how he could
sanction the executions. He replied, "Look, in this
thing either you kill first, or else you get killed."[1]

Only a couple of days after he took control of
La Cabaña, Guevara's parents and siblings visited
him. Soon afterward, Gadea arrived with their
daughter, Hildita. Guevara told his wife that he had
met another woman during the war. Although the
two decided to divorce, Guevara often invited his
daughter to visit him at La Cabaña.

## Shaping a New Government

While Guevara was overseeing the trials at La
Cabaña, he also was working behind the scenes
to help shape the country's political direction.

Although Castro had stated repeatedly during the war that he was not leading a Communist revolution, he had Guevara work to cement ties with Cuba's Communist Party. As chief of the Department of Training of the Revolutionary Armed Forces, Guevara also began introducing Communist ideas to the country's soldiers.

On February 7, 1959, a special clause in the new Cuban constitution granted Cuban citizenship to anyone who had fought in the revolution for two

---

**Trials at La Cabaña**

As supreme prosecutor at La Cabaña, Guevara determined the fate of thousands of accused war criminals who were charged with informing the Cuban army of the revolution's movements or of torturing revolutionary soldiers. In order to remain neutral, Guevara never met with the defendants and did not attend their trials. Instead, he spoke with the judges who sat on the trials. He made his decisions based on the evidence they presented. In 1962, *New York Times* reporter R. Hart Phillips described a late-night trial at La Cabaña that she was allowed to witness:

> The three judges sat at a table on a platform. Just below was the prisoner guarded by two soldiers. It was a dismal scene. The masonry walls were peeling, the chairs were wobbly and there was only a dim light. . . . A couple of witnesses testified that the prisoner had betrayed a revolutionary to the Batista authorities. The judges sent out for Coca-Cola. . . . There were no defense witnesses. The defense attorney made no defense but apologized to the court for defending the prisoner.[2]

Although Phillips did not remain for the end of the trial, she later learned that the prisoner had been sentenced to death. He was shot a few hours later.

or more years and had served as a comandante for at least a year. The law meant that Guevara was now a citizen of Cuba. Only a month later, exhausted from the two-year-long guerrilla war, Guevara suffered a severe and prolonged asthma attack. He was ordered by doctors to rest in the nearby beach town of Tarará. The town had formerly housed many wealthy Batista supporters, and Guevara took up residence in the luxurious home of a member of the former regime. When a magazine article mentioned his new living situation, Guevara published an explanation:

**No Special Treatment**

Even while in a position of power in Cuba, Guevara refused to accept special treatment for himself or his family. For example, his family was given additional food above and beyond the government rations that everyone else received. But he put a stop to the benefit, despite the fact that his family barely had enough to eat. He also refused to allow his wife to use the car to get groceries or to take a sick child to the hospital. He insisted that the car was for official government use only and that she must take the bus, like everyone else.

> I had to occupy a house that had belonged to a batistiano
> [supporter of Batista] because my salary as an officer of the
> Rebel Army is $125.00, which does not permit me to rent
> one sufficiently large for my entire household. . . . I chose the
> simplest. . . . I promise . . . the people of Cuba that I shall
> abandon it as soon as I have recovered my health.[3]

By May, Guevara was well enough to leave Tarará.

*On June 2, 1959, Guevara married Aleida March
in a civil ceremony at La Cabaña.*

On June 2, 1959, he married Aleida March. For the
small civil ceremony, he wore his everyday clothes—a
green military uniform and black beret. Over the
next six years, the couple would have four children:
Aleida, Camilo, Celia, and Ernesto.

### NEW ROLES

Only ten days after the wedding, Guevara left
Cuba for an extended trip abroad. In three months,
he visited 14 countries, including Japan, Yugoslavia,

India, Egypt, Pakistan, and other countries with which Cuba wanted to establish diplomatic and trade relationships. A few weeks after Guevara's return to Cuba in September 1959, Castro put him in charge of the new Department of Industries at the Instituto Nacional de Reforma Agraria (INRA), or National Institute of Agrarian Reform. The department had been created to implement an agrarian reform law that limited the size of plantations and redistributed some land to peasants.

Only weeks later, Guevara was given another role. In addition to his position at the INRA, he was selected to serve as president of the National Bank of Cuba. The two positions gave Guevara nearly complete control of the country's finances and input in its economic policies. Despite his new positions, he admitted to another government official who was hesitant to take on a position with him at the bank, "I don't know anything about banks, either, and I'm the president. But when the revolution names you to a post, you have to accept it, and then do it well."[4] As bank president,

**Assassination Attempts**

Within the first few years after the victory of the Cuban Revolution, there was at least one attempt, and possibly more, to assassinate Guevara. As a result, Guevara instituted several security measures. He took a different route to work every day, carried a cigar box filled with grenades in his car, and required visitors to the Ministry of Industry to be searched.

Guevara was in charge of signing the nation's currency—he wrote his name as simply Che. He also was responsible for overseeing the development of a volunteer program. And on Sunday mornings, he volunteered to harvest sugar cane or unload ships.

Determined to end Cuban dependence on sugar exports to the United States, Guevara worked to industrialize the country and instituted a program of rapid nationalization. To achieve this, the government took control of the country's privately owned industries, including many owned by Americans, and brought more land under state ownership. Guevara also helped Cuba establish a relationship with the Communist Soviet Union, which agreed to buy Cuban sugar and provide the country with machinery and factories. In late 1960, Guevara embarked on a two-month trip to the Communist countries of Eastern Europe, China, and the Soviet Union. In each country, he was received as a hero.

## Minister of Industry

On February 24, 1961, Guevara's role in the Cuban economy was expanded as he was named the country's first minister of industry. Despite his increasing workload, which often kept him at the office until 3:00 a.m., he refused to accept a salary for his new position. Instead, he supported his family on the $125 a month he made as a comandante in the army. Putting in 18- to 20-hour days, Guevara had little time for his wife and children. On the rare occasions that he was home, he spent much of it in his office reading and studying. He would take time to play with his children, though, on Sunday afternoons.

During Guevara's four years as minister of industry, he continued the policies of nationalization and industrialization that he had begun earlier. He also attempted to diversify Cuba's economy by cutting back on sugar production and cultivating new crops. He insisted that all state-owned companies share their profits and that people work for "moral incentives" (the knowledge that they were helping to better their country), rather than for material rewards, such as paid vacations. His economic program was a failure, however. With

### The Cuban Missile Crisis

The Cuban Missile Crisis brought the world closer to nuclear war than ever before—or since. In October 1962, the United States detected the presence of Soviet nuclear missiles in Cuba. In response, President John F. Kennedy declared a naval blockade against Cuba and demanded the removal of the missiles, which could have hit nearly any location in the eastern United States. For six days, people around the world waited as American nuclear installations were placed on high alert. Finally, after tense negotiations, the Soviets backed down, agreeing to remove the weapons. In return, the United States promised never to invade Cuba and secretly agreed to remove its own nuclear weapons from Turkey.

a US trade embargo in place against the now openly Communist country, Cuba was experiencing severe shortages of goods by March 1962. Basic necessities such as rice, beans, milk, chicken, and toothpaste were rationed.

That year, Guevara and the Cuban government accepted a Soviet offer to place nuclear missiles on the island to prevent a US invasion of Cuba. That decision provoked the Cuban Missile Crisis in October. This intense standoff with the United States ended with the Soviet Union ultimately agreeing to withdraw the missiles. Angered, Guevara told a reporter, "If the rockets had remained, we would have used them all and directed them against the very heart of the United States, including New York, in our defense against aggression."[6]

*President John F. Kennedy announced a blockade of Cuba
in a televised speech made on October 22, 1962.*

*In 1962, Guevara served as minister of industry in the Cuban government and continued to promote revolutionary movements around the world.*

# FAILURE IN AFRICA

Almost immediately after Castro came to power, Guevara began promoting the spread of revolution to all of Latin America. Beginning in 1959, the Cuban government provided support for revolutions in Panama, Nicaragua, the Dominican Republic, Haiti, Guatemala, and Venezuela, but none had been successful. By 1962, Cuba had formed a training camp to school potential revolutionaries from around Latin America in the techniques of guerrilla warfare. Guevara became one of the leaders of the school and mentored the future revolutionaries.

According to Hilda Gadea's brother Ricardo, who participated in the Cuban training camp, "Of all the leaders, Che was the most charismatic, sensitive, and involved, as a Latin American. He understood us, knew our difficulties, and helped us overcome many of our problems."[1]

In the wake of the October 1962 Cuban Missile Crisis, Guevara was even more determined to spread revolution not only to Latin America but also to Africa. He also set his mind on joining in the fight, but he had not yet decided where.

In December 1964, Guevara traveled to New York to attend a meeting of the United Nations General Assembly. After delivering a speech in which he accused the United States of interfering in the affairs of other countries, Guevara embarked on a three-month trip to Africa. From December 1964 to February 1965, he traveled to Algeria, Mali,

*At a 1964 United Nations assembly, Guevara delivered a speech that accused the United States of interfering in other countries' affairs.*

Congo-Brazzaville, Guinea, Ghana, and Algeria, encouraging revolution against imperialist powers. During the course of his trip, he met with Laurent Kabila, the Congolese revolutionary leader. Kabila was leading a guerrilla campaign against the newly independent country's government. Guevara secretly offered Cuba's help in the form of instructors and weapons.

To conclude his African trip, Guevara traveled to Algeria. On February 25, he delivered a speech in

which he was critical of the Soviet Union. He said it was not doing enough to aid developing nations that were struggling to establish Communist societies. On March 15, Guevara returned to Cuba and was immediately ushered into a long, secret meeting with Castro. Over the next two weeks, Guevara began to withdraw from public life in Cuba. While rumors of the cause of his disappearance circulated around the world, only a handful of people realized that Guevara had left the country on April 1.

### DISASTER IN THE CONGO

In disguise, with his face and head shaved and wearing glasses, Guevara was able to leave Cuba secretly. For nearly three weeks, he traveled a winding route through several countries, including the Soviet Union and Egypt. He arrived at his destination of Dar es Salaam, Tanzania, on April 19. He had made the decision to join the fight in the Congo, which was across Lake Tanganyika from Tanzania. Browsing through a Swahili dictionary, Guevara gave himself and his companions new names. Choosing from Swahili numbers, he was "Tato" (three). Guevara remained in disguise, revealing his true identity only to a few, which included Kabila, who had not known that Guevara would be coming. It was feared that the conflict might escalate if Guevara's presence were made known and that countries such as the United States would become involved.

By the end of April, Guevara had crossed Lake Tanganyika and arrived at the camp of the Congolese rebels. He found the Congolese to be disorganized and undisciplined. He was able to communicate with only a few of the leaders, who spoke French, while most of the fighters spoke only tribal languages or Swahili. Despite the

## Looking for Guevara

By the end of April 1965, only a few weeks after Guevara had disappeared from public life, rumors began to spread regarding his whereabouts. Some people thought he might have been jailed or placed under house arrest. Others believed he might have been hospitalized for a severe asthma attack. There were even reports that he was in a mental institution after suffering a psychiatric breakdown. More extreme stories reported that Guevara and Castro had had a falling out and that Guevara had been exiled, punished, or even shot.

Castro issued this statement on April 20:

*The only thing I can tell you is that Comandante Guevara is always where he will be most useful to the revolution, and that relations between him and me are the best.[2]*

Some people began to suspect the truth: that Guevara was leading a revolution in another part of the world. However, they were not sure where. Reports placed him in the Dominican Republic, Vietnam, or Brazil. The Cuban government did nothing to stop the rumors. Instead, they added to the confusion by leaking false information.

language barrier, he tried to set up a training program and to establish a more permanent base camp. He was told, though, that he could do nothing until the base commander, who was away in Tanzania, returned. As more Cubans began to arrive in camp, Guevara gave them lessons in French, Swahili, and "general culture" in order to fight the boredom that had begun to set in. He also served as a doctor to the peasants in the area. Soon, Guevara and his Cuban fighters suffered from malaria and other infections contracted in the tropical environment. In addition, Guevara had to deal with his asthma almost constantly.

By May, Guevara had been given the authorization to establish a new camp, and he set out to build it at the top of a large grassy plateau. On May 22, Guevara's Cuban friend Osmany Cienfuegos arrived in camp with sad news. Guevara recorded the news in his diary:

**His Mother's Illness**

Guevara's mother died of cancer on May 18, 1965, four days before he received word of her illness. On May 10, she had been hospitalized at the exclusive Stapler Clinic in Buenos Aires. But the family soon learned that she was not welcome there because of her son's Communist philosophy. Moved to another clinic, she was left wondering about her son and his whereabouts.

*Telephone callers from Buenos Aires had revealed that my mother was very ill, in a tone that led one to suppose that they were simply paving the way for a further announcement. . . . I had to spend a month in uncertainty, awaiting the outcome of something that was already suspected, but in the hope that there had been a mistake—until, finally, confirmation of my mother's death arrived.[3]*

## A Short Fight

In late June, Guevara finally received permission to send his force into battle. He was not allowed to join the combat, though. Approximately 40 Cubans and 160 Congolese rebels and Rwandan allies attacked Fort Bendera, which was defended by 300 soldiers. The attack was a disaster. Many of the Congolese and Rwandan rebels fled or refused to fight. The Cubans

**Another Fight?**

Even as Guevara prepared to evacuate his troops and leave the Congo, he contemplated staying to continue the fight. On the other side of the country, more than 900 miles (1,450 km) away, another rebel group under different leadership also struggled against the Congolese government. Guevara considered attempting to cross the jungle to reach them. But at his Cuban comrades' insistence that he leave, he was "deeply pained at the thought of . . . leaving behind defenseless peasants and armed men whose poor battle sense left them effectively defenseless, defeated and with a feeling of betrayal."[4]

stayed for the battle, and four men were killed. Afterward, Guevara tried to convince Kabila to let him set up a training program and a supply and communications network. He received little response.

By August, Guevara no longer cared whether he had Kabila's permission, and he left for the front lines. He was able to organize a few ambushes in which the rebels fought, rather than fled. He also met with a number of peasants, giving them vegetable seeds, malaria drugs, and penicillin.

In mid-October, the Congolese army began to encircle Guevara and his men. When the rebel camp was attacked on October 24, Guevara ordered a retreat. In the confusion, large stores of weapons, food, and equipment were lost. He blamed himself for being taken by surprise.

In November, Guevara received a letter from Castro, who had

**Coup in the Congo**

On November 24, 1965, only days after Guevara had left the country, Joseph Mobutu, commander in chief of the Congolese armed forces, took over the presidency in a coup. He then changed the country's name to Zaire.

Laurent Kabila, who had failed to overthrow the Congolese government with Guevara in 1965, led a successful revolt and became president in 1997. After restoring the country's name to the Democratic Republic of the Congo, Kabila faced an outbreak of fighting that became a five-year civil war. Assassinated in January 2001, he was succeeded by his son Joseph, who continued to deal with unrest into 2010.

been continuously updated on the progress of
the revolution. In the letter, Castro said Guevara
should "do everything except what is absurd,"
consider withdrawing if his presence had become
"pointless and unjustifiable," and "avoid any
annihilation."[5] Guevara, however, was not willing to
leave the Congolese unless they asked him. In mid-
November, they did so, and Guevara ordered the
Cubans to evacuate.

*Guevara went to the Congo in 1965 to support a guerilla movement.*

*Guevara met the people of Bolivia while trying to spark a revolution there.*

# ULTIMATE DEFEAT

*A*fter withdrawing from the Congo, Guevara was taken to the Cuban embassy in Dar es Salaam, Tanzania. Ill and fatigued, he had lost more than 40 pounds (18 kg) during his time in the Congo. As he recovered, Guevara

contemplated where to go next. Before leaving
Cuba, he had given Castro a farewell letter in
which he formally resigned all of his positions in
the Cuban government and his Cuban citizenship.
Castro read the letter publicly in October 1965. The
Cuban dictator tried to convince Guevara to return
to the country, but Guevara's pride kept him from
doing so.

In February or March of 1966, Guevara moved
to Prague, Czechoslovakia. Once again, he began
making plans for a new revolution—this time in
the South American country of Bolivia. Unlike
the Congo, Bolivia was not already in the midst of
revolution. Despite the fact that
many peasants lived in poverty, the
country's president, René Barrientos,
was very popular. Still, Guevara was
determined to spark a revolution in
the country. He saw it as a starting
point for revolutions in Argentina
and the rest of Latin America. With
Castro's help, Guevara secretly
returned to Cuba in July. He selected
a team of 12 Cubans to join him in
his new venture.

**A Secret Good-bye**

In order to maintain the
secrecy of his Bolivian
operation, Guevara could
not openly say good-bye
to his children. Instead,
they were brought to him
while he was in disguise.
The children did not rec-
ognize their father, who
was introduced to them
as their Uncle Ramón.

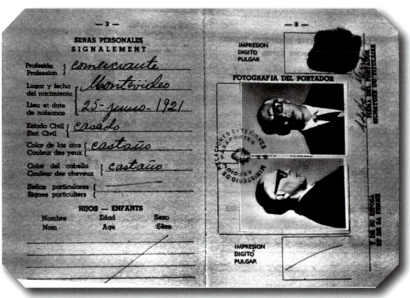

*The fake passport Guevara used showed him disguised as a balding man from Uruguay.*

## Into Bolivia

Before leaving for Bolivia, Guevara sent some of his top guerrillas to the country. The men established a base of operations in the forest-covered hills of the Ñancahuazú region in the southeastern part of the country. In early November 1966, Guevara arrived at the base disguised as a heavy-set, balding, middle-aged Uruguayan. Soon, more Cubans began to arrive at the camp. So did some Bolivians, most of whom were part of the Bolivian Communist Party.

On February 1, 1967, Guevara left four of his 33 men in camp. He took the rest on what was planned to be a two-week training march. The men quickly became lost, however. They spent the next 48 days cutting their way through dense forest with machetes, crossing swollen rivers, and hiking in and out of canyons. Along the way, they were plagued by torrential rains, swarming mosquitoes, and constant hunger and thirst.

## The Battle Begins

The men finally returned to camp on March 20, weak and exhausted. They could not rest, however, as a government plane circled the area. After capturing two Bolivian deserters, the Bolivian army had learned of the guerrilla camp. The day that Guevara's group returned to camp, one of the guerrillas killed a Bolivian soldier patrolling the area. Guevara knew that a response from the army would come quickly.

On March 23, fighting broke out as the guerrillas ambushed an

### Guerilla Survivors

Most of the Cubans with Guevara in Bolivia were there out of loyalty to their comandante—not because they believed in the Bolivian revolution. Only three of the Cubans, along with two Bolivians, survived the experience. Crossing more than 500 miles (805 km) of the wild Bolivian countryside, they were often pursued closely by the Bolivian army. They were able to escape into the Andes Mountains and reach Chile, where they were rescued and flown to Cuba.

army patrol near their base. The first victory in the Bolivian revolution went to the rebels. They killed seven soldiers and took another 14 as prisoners. Within days, however, the Bolivian government mobilized its forces. In early April, the main guerrilla camp was overrun, but the guerrillas were not there. They had moved out and would continue to be on the move for the next six months.

Guevara's force now numbered 47; the Bolivian army had 20,000 troops at its command. Despite being outnumbered, the guerrillas were able to hold their own against the army throughout much of the spring.

## A Fateful Decision

On April 18, Guevara decided to split his small force into two columns. He headed one column to take the village of Muyupampa. The other, headed by a Cuban rebel given the alias Joaquín, remained behind with the sick. The plan was to meet up again in three days. When Guevara's column arrived at Muyupampa, however, they discovered that the Bolivian army was already there. Two noncombatants, who were carrying out other work for Guevara and had traveled with him to the town, had been captured by the Bolivian army. After being threatened and beaten, they had confirmed Guevara's presence in the country, which until then had only been suspected.

From Muyupampa, Guevara attempted to rejoin Joaquín's group. Their radios had stopped working though, and the men were unable to make contact. The two columns spent the next four months searching for each other. As they wandered the area, Guevara's column was constantly chased by the Bolivian army. In several battles, some of Guevara's men were killed. He tried to enlist peasant support but found none. In many cases, peasants informed the army of his whereabouts.

In May and June, Guevara suffered several illnesses and severe asthma attacks. He began riding mules or horses in order to keep up with his men. On July 6, Guevara ordered an attack on the town of Samaipata. The objective was to obtain asthma

### Capturing Guevara

By the time Guevara was captured, the CIA had been tracking him for more than a decade. As soon as the Cuban revolutionary's presence in Bolivia was discovered, the United States sent a group of special forces to train the Bolivian army. In addition, two CIA agents were dispatched to the country.

One was Felix Rodríguez, a Cuban exile whose family had fled the island during the Cuban Revolution. Rodríguez had wanted Guevara evacuated to Panama for questioning but later wrote of the execution, "It was a tremendously emotional moment for me. I no longer hated him. His moment of truth had come, and he was conducting himself like a man."[1]

medication and other supplies. Although the rebels succeeded in taking the town, they did not get asthma medicine and Guevara continued to suffer.

In response to the attack on Samaipata, the Bolivian army launched an offensive. In a battle on July 30, Guevara lost his tape recorder. He had been using it to decode messages from Havana, but he was now on his own. Guevara's men grew weaker by the day and spent much of their time scrounging for food and water. Malnourished,

---

### Che's Children

After Guevara's death, his children received a letter he had written to them before leaving for the Congo. In it, he wrote:

*If one day you must read this letter, it will be because I am no longer among you. . . . Grow up as good revolutionaries. . . . Above all, try always to be able to feel deeply any injustice committed against any person in any part of the world. It is the most beautiful quality of a revolutionary.*[2]

As his children grew up, they tried to heed their father's words. Guevara's oldest daughter, Hildita, married (and later divorced) a Mexican guerrilla. Later, she became a researcher at Cuba's La Casa de las Américas. She put together a bibliography of her father's works. Sons Camilo and Ernesto both spent time studying in Moscow. Afterward, Camilo worked at Cuba's ministry of fisheries before operating the Che Guevara Studies Center in Havana. Ernesto worked at a state-run electronics company. Daughter Aleida spent time in Nicaragua and Angola and became a pediatrician. She also travels the world speaking about her father. Celia became a veterinarian.

All of the children still help to perpetuate their father's memory. In Cuba, people sometimes stop them in the street to hug them and tourists are thrilled to meet them.

they also began to experience dizziness and fainting spells.

In early September, Guevara heard a radio report that a rebel column had been defeated and killed in the south on August 31. At first, he refused to believe that the army had found Joaquín's group, but he eventually had to accept the truth. His second column, representing approximately one-third of his rebel army, was gone.

## END OF THE REVOLUTION

By this time, Guevara had wandered into the mountains of the Vallegrande province. The Bolivian army had already established a base of operations in the region, and was alerted to the approaching rebels. On September 26, after being ambushed in the tiny town of La Higuera, the rebels took refuge in a canyon. Two days later, still in hiding, Guevara wrote of their precarious situation in his diary, "A day of anxiety which at one moment seemed to be our last one . . . . The possibilities of escaping would have been remote if they had discovered us."[3]

On September 30, Guevara and his men began to make their way deeper into the canyon. By October 7, they had reached a steep ravine near La

Higuera known as the Quebrada del Yuro. The next morning, the rebels—now numbering only 17—found their position surrounded by soldiers. The only way out was to fight. The battle began at 1:10 p.m. and lasted just over two hours. A number of the guerrillas were killed, and Guevara was wounded in the leg. A Bolivian guerrilla tried to help him out of the canyon, but the two were spotted by Bolivian soldiers. With the soldiers' guns aimed at him, Guevara called out, "Don't shoot. I am Che Guevara. I am worth more to you alive than dead."[4]

With his hands bound, Guevara was forced to walk to La Higuera. He was then thrown onto the dirt floor of a schoolhouse. The next afternoon, he was executed.

## Che Vive

On October 10, Guevara's dead body was placed on display in a hospital in the town of Vallegrande. Reporters and photographers were invited to see his body and confirm his death. The first official reports state that the revolutionary had been killed in combat, but it soon became clear that he had been captured alive and killed by the Bolivian army.

After the public display of Guevara's body, it disappeared. The Bolivian army claimed it had been cremated. This remained the official story until 1995, when an army general confessed that the body had been secretly buried. A search for his remains was subsequently carried out. In June 1997, his body was found. It was easily identified because it had no hands. Guevara's hands had been cut off after his death so that his fingerprints could be analyzed. The body was returned to Cuba.

In October 1997, Guevara was honored in a public ceremony. At the ceremony, Castro said,

**In Hollywood's Spotlight**

In the first decade of the twenty-first century, Hollywood cashed in on Guevara's enduring popularity. In 2004, *The Motorcycle Diaries,* starring Gael Garcia Bernal, was released. It was based on Guevara's journey through Latin America while he was still in medical school. Four years later, Benicio del Toro starred in *Che,* which chronicles Guevara's experiences in the Cuban and Bolivian revolutions. Both movies are in Spanish and have English subtitles.

> *Those who wanted to kill him, to make him disappear, were not able to understand that he would leave an indelible footprint in history and that his luminous prophet's gaze would transform him into a symbol for all the earth's poor in their millions upon millions.*[5]

Castro was right. Almost immediately after Guevara's death, many viewed him as a martyred hero. He became a symbol of revolutionary fervor and personal rebellion. The words Che vive! (Che lives!) appeared on posters in college dormitories and on banners at student demonstrations. In Asia, Africa, and Latin America, Guevara's name was invoked as new revolutionaries began their own guerrilla wars.

Now, more than 40 years after Guevara's death, his presence can still be found. His image is widely printed on T-shirts, key chains, baseball hats, posters, and even cigars. They are sold in the countries he denounced as imperialist. Some people oppose such displays, saying that Guevara was nothing more than a murderer. In Cuba, however, where the revolutionary government he helped bring to power is still in place, schoolchildren begin their day by proclaiming that they want to be like Che.

Whether glorified or vilified, Che Guevara is certainly remembered, helping to fulfill a hope he expressed shortly before his death: "Wherever death may surprise us, let it be welcome, provided that this, our battle cry, may have reached some receptive ear."[6]

*Cuban schoolchildren honor Guevara as a national hero.*

# TIMELINE

| 1928 | 1930 | 1947 |
|------|------|------|
| Ernesto Guevara de la Serna is born in Rosario, Argentina, on June 14; some sources say May 14. | On May 2, Guevara suffers his first attack of asthma, a disease he struggles with for the rest of his life. | Guevara enrolls in the University of Buenos Aires to study medicine. |

| 1955 | 1955 | 1956 |
|------|------|------|
| Guevara meets Fidel Castro for the first time during the late summer. | Guevara marries Hilda Gadea on August 18. Their daughter is born on February 15, 1956. | On November 25, Guevara, Castro, and 80 guerrillas board the *Granma* and arrive in Cuba on December 2. |

### 1952

In January, Guevara and Alberto Granado leave on a tour of South America.

### 1953

On April 11, Guevara passes his last exam to become a doctor. In July, he leaves on another Latin American tour.

### 1953

On December 24, Guevara arrives in Guatemala City. He becomes friends with a number of Cuban exiles.

### 1957

Guevara is promoted to comandante, the highest rank in the revolutionary army, on July 22.

### 1958

On August 31, Guevara leads 148 rebels toward Las Villas province for the final campaign of the Cuban Revolution.

### 1959

On January 1, Cuba's president, Fulgencio Batista, flees the country and the revolutionary army gains control of Cuba.

# TIMELINE

| 1959 | 1959 | 1959 |
|---|---|---|
| A special law is passed on February 7, making Guevara a Cuban citizen. | After divorcing Gadea, Guevara marries Aleida March on June 2. | On October 7, Guevara is appointed head of the department of industries at the National Institute of Agrarian Reform. |

| 1965 | 1965 | 1965 |
|---|---|---|
| On March 15, Guevara drops out of public view and secretly travels to the Congo and attempts to aid a revolution under Laurent Kabila. | On October 3, Castro publicly reads a farewell letter in which Guevara resigns his Cuban citizenship. | After a disastrous experience in the Congo, Guevara leaves the country on November 21. |

## 1959

On November 26, Guevara becomes president of the National Bank of Cuba.

## 1961

Guevara becomes Cuba's first minister of industry on February 24.

## 1964

Guevara travels to New York and speaks before the UN General Assembly on December 11 before leaving for a tour of Africa.

## 1966

Guevara departs for Bolivia on October 23. His goal is to spark a Bolivian revolution.

## 1967

Guevara separates his forces in Bolivia into two columns on April 18.

## 1967

Guevara is captured by Bolivian forces on October 8. He is executed the next day.

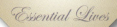
# Essential Facts

### Date of Birth

June 14, 1928 (other sources state he was born May 14, 1928)

### Place of Birth

Rosario, Argentina

### Date of Death

October 9, 1967

### Parents

Ernesto Guevara Lynch and Celia de la Serna

### Education

Escuela San Martín, Alta Gracia, Argentina

Colegio Nacional Deán Funes, Córdoba, Argentina

University of Buenos Aires, Argentina

### Marriages

Hilda Gadea (August 18, 1955, to June 2, 1959)

Aleida March (June 2, 1959)

### Children

Hilda, Aleida, Camilo, Celia, and Ernesto

## Career Highlights

❖ In 1955, Guevara joined Castro in the Cuban Revolution. Guevara reached the rank of comandante in the revolutionary army.

❖ After the successful capture of Cuba, Guevara served as head of the department of industries at the National Institute of Agrarian Reform, president of the National Bank of Cuba, and minister of industry.

❖ In 1965, Guevara attempted to assist a revolution in the Congo. In 1967, he attempted to organize a revolution in Bolivia.

## Societal Contribution

After traveling through the nations of South America, Guevara saw the poverty of the continent's peasants. He dedicated the rest of his life to fighting revolutions aimed at undermining the power such countries wielded.

## Conflicts

❖ Guevara struggled with asthma. As an adult, he pushed himself to march up and down mountains during guerrilla campaigns—often without medication.

❖ In the Congo and Bolivia Guevara often dealt with deserters and informers.

## Quote

"The soul of a people is reflected in the sick in the hospitals, the men in custody at police stations or the anxious pedestrian with whom one enters into conversation."—*Che Guevara*

# GLOSSARY

**agrarian**
Having to do with land and its ownership or division.

**bilge**
The lowest internal part of a ship's hull, where the bottom curves up to meet the sides.

**column**
Troops or military vehicles moving in successive lines in the same direction.

**communism**
A form of government in which industry and agriculture are owned and controlled by the state, with the ultimate goal of sharing all goods equally among the people.

**coup**
The sudden and sometimes violent overthrow of a government, often by the military, which then takes power.

**court martial**
A military court where cases are heard for those charged with breaking military law.

**embargo**
An official government-ordered restriction or ban on trade with a specific country or of a specific item.

**exile**
A person who is living away from his or her native country, either by choice or because he or she has been forced to do so.

**garrison**
A building that is occupied by troops defending a town.

**guerrilla**
A member of an unofficial military, operating outside government control, usually for political purposes and often operating in small strike forces.

**imperialism**
The practice in which one country spreads its authority by dominating the economy or politics of another, usually weaker, country.

**industrialize**
To develop a nation's industry, or large-scale production of goods.

**leper**
Someone who has leprosy, an infectious tropical disease caused by bacteria that affects the skin and nerves, causing sores, white scabs, tissue damage, and deformity.

**malaria**
A disease that causes severe, recurring chills and fever and is spread by a parasite passed to humans by mosquitoes.

**mercenary**
A soldier who is paid to fight for a force other than his or her own country's army.

**nationalization**
The transfer of control from privately owned businesses, industry, and land to the government.

**offensive**
A military attack.

**pampa**
A South American grassland that covers a large, flat area and has no trees.

**propaganda**
Information, sometimes distorted, that is distributed by a government or organization to spread a particular idea and advance its cause.

**socialist**
A person who believes in the political system of socialism, which holds that private property should be eliminated and the production and distribution of goods should be controlled by society as a whole.

**viceroy**
A governor of a country or province who rules as the representative of a sovereign.

## ADDITIONAL RESOURCES

### SELECTED BIBLIOGRAPHY

Anderson, Jon Lee. *Che Guevara: A Revolutionary Life*. New York: Grove Press, 1997. Print.

Castañeda, Jorge G. *Compañero: The Life and Death of Che Guevara*. Trans. Marina Castañeda. New York: Alfred A. Knopf, 1997. Print.

Gadea, Hilda. *Ernesto: A Memoir of Che Guevara*. Trans. Carmen Molina and Walter Bradbury. Garden City, NY: Doubleday & Company, 1972. Print.

Guevara, Ernesto Che. *The African Dream: The Diaries of the Revolutionary War in the Congo*. Trans. Patrick Camiller. New York: Grove Press, 2000. Print.

Guevara, Ernesto Che. *The Motorcycle Diaries: Notes on a Latin American Journey*. Trans. Alexandra Keeble. New York: Ocean Press, 2004. Print.

### FURTHER READINGS

Crompton, Samuel. *Che Guevara: The Making of a Revolutionary*. Pleasantville, NY: Gareth Stevens, 2009. Print.

Miller, Calvin Craig. *Che Guevara: In Search of Revolution*. Greensboro, NC: Morgan Reynolds, 2006. Print.

Uschan, Michael. *Che Guevara, Revolutionary*. Farmington Hills, MI: Lucent Books, 2007. Print.

### WEB LINKS

To learn more about Che Guevara, visit ABDO Publishing Company online at **www.abdopublishing.com**. Web sites about Che Guevara are featured on our Book Links page. These links are routinely monitored and updated to provide the most current information available.

## Places to Visit

**Cuban Foundation Museum**
352 South Nova Road, Daytona Beach, FL 32114
386–255–0285
www.moas.org/cuban%20art.html
Located within Daytona Beach's Museum of Arts and Sciences, the Cuban Foundation Museum houses more than 200 objects, including paintings, sculptures, furniture, documents, and maps. These items reflect Cuban history from 1659 to 1959, when Castro took over the country. Many of the museum's objects were donated to the city of Daytona Beach by Castro's predecessor, Fulgencio Batista, who had a second home in the city during the 1940s and 1950s.

**El Museo del Barrio**
1230 Fifth Avenue, New York, NY 10029
212–831–7272
www.elmuseo.org
El Museo del Barrio highlights the art and culture of Latin America and the islands of the Caribbean. It features works of art from contemporary Latin Americans, as well as indigenous artifacts dating to before Columbus's arrival in the Americas. In addition, the museum offers concerts, cultural celebrations, and other special events.

**Museo del Che Guevara**
Avellaneda 501 – Barrio Carlos Pellegrini, Alta Gracia, Córdoba, Argentina
00–54–03547–428579
Located at one of the homes in which the Guevara family lived in Alta Gracia, the Museo del Che Guevara was opened in 2001 to display pictures, furniture, books, and even bicycles from Guevara's youth. Another home in which Guevara's family lived is located just down the road. Visitors to Alta Gracia can also travel to the nearby city of Córdoba, where Guevara spent his high school years.

# SOURCE NOTES

**Chapter 1. Triumph in Cuba**

1. Ernesto Che Guevara. *Reminiscences of the Cuban Revolutionary War*. Trans. Victoria Ortiz. New York: Monthly Review Press, 1968. Print. 251.

2. Ibid. 252.

3. Joanne Fowler. "The Way of Che." *People.com*. People Magazine. 25 Sept. 2000. Web. 11 May 2010.

4. Ernesto Che Guevara. *Reminiscences of the Cuban Revolutionary War*. Trans. Victoria Ortiz. New York: Monthly Review Press, 1968. Print. 254.

**Chapter 2. An Argentine Youth**

1. Jorge G. Castañeda. *Compañero: The Life and Death of Che Guevara*. Trans. Marina Castañeda. New York: Alfred A. Knopf, 1997. Print. 13.

2. Dolores Moyano Martín. "A Memoir of the Young Guevara: The Making of a Revolutionary." *New York Times*. 18 Aug. 1968. Print. 48.

3. Ibid.

4. Jon Lee Anderson. *Che Guevara: A Revolutionary Life*. New York: Grove Press, 1997. Print. 28.

5. Ibid. 34.

**Chapter 3. College Life**

1. Ernesto Guevara Lynch. *Young Che: Memories of Che Guevara by His Father*. Trans. Lucía Álvarez de Toledo. New York: Vintage Books, 2007. Print. 176.

2. Ibid. 168.

3. Ibid. 171.

4. Jorge G. Castañeda. *Compañero: The Life and Death of Che Guevara*. Trans. Marina Castañeda. New York: Alfred A. Knopf, 1997. Print. 38.

5. Dolores Moyano Martín. "A Memoir of the Young Guevara: The Making of a Revolutionary." *New York Times*. 18 Aug. 1968. Print. 61.

6. Jon Lee Anderson. *Che Guevara: A Revolutionary Life*. New York: Grove Press, 1997. Print. 67.

7. Ibid.

**Chapter 4. *The Motorcycle Diaries***

1. Ernesto Che Guevara. *The Motorcycle Diaries: Notes on a Latin American Journey*. Trans. Alexandra Keeble. New York: Ocean Press, 2004. Print. 53–54.

2. Ibid. 78.

3. Jorge G. Castañeda. *Compañero: The Life and Death of Che Guevara*. Trans. Marina Castañeda. New York: Alfred A. Knopf, 1997. Print. 45.

4. Ernesto Che Guevara. *The Motorcycle Diaries: Notes on a Latin American Journey*. Trans. Alexandra Keeble. New York: Ocean Press, 2004. Print. 93.

5. Jon Lee Anderson. *Che Guevara: A Revolutionary Life*. New York: Grove Press, 1997. Print. 117.

6. Ernesto Che Guevara. *The Motorcycle Diaries: Notes on a Latin American Journey*. Trans. Alexandra Keeble. New York: Ocean Press, 2004. Print. 157.

7. Ibid. 32.

**Chapter 5. Becoming Che**

1. Ernesto Che Guevara. *Back on the Road: A Journey through Latin America*. Trans. Patrick Camiller. New York: Grove Press, 2001. Print. 3.

2. Hilda Gadea. *Ernesto: A Memoir of Che Guevara*. Trans. Carmen Molina and Walter Bradbury. Garden City, NY: Doubleday & Company, 1972. Print. 2.

3. Karl Marx and Friedrich Engels. *The Communist Manifesto*. 1888. Trans. Samuel Moore. New York: Penguin Classics, 2002. Print. 258.

4. Ernesto Che Guevara. *Back on the Road: A Journey through Latin America*. Trans. Patrick Camiller. New York: Grove Press, 2001. Print. 99.

5. Daniel James. *Che Guevara: A Biography*. 1969. New York: Cooper Square Press, 2001. Print. 86.

6. Jon Lee Anderson. *Che Guevara: A Revolutionary Life*. New York: Grove Press, 1997. Print. 195.

## SOURCE NOTES CONTINUED

**Chapter 6. The Revolutionary**

1. Ernesto Che Guevara. *Reminiscences of the Cuban Revolutionary War*. Trans. Victoria Ortiz. New York: Monthly Review Press, 1968. Print. 44.

2. Jon Lee Anderson. *Che Guevara: A Revolutionary Life*. New York: Grove Press, 1997. Print. 219.

3. Ernesto Che Guevara. *Reminiscences of the Cuban Revolutionary War*. Trans. Victoria Ortiz. New York: Monthly Review Press, 1968. Print. 54.

4. Jon Lee Anderson. *Che Guevara: A Revolutionary Life*. New York: Grove Press, 1997. Print. 228.

5. Ibid. 309.

6. Ernesto Che Guevara. *Reminiscences of the Cuban Revolutionary War*. Trans. Victoria Ortiz. New York: Monthly Review Press, 1968. Print. 108.

7. Ibid. 138.

8. Jon Lee Anderson. *Che Guevara: A Revolutionary Life*. New York: Grove Press, 1997. Print. 305–306.

9. Jorge G. Castañeda. *Compañero: The Life and Death of Che Guevara*. Trans. Marina Castañeda. New York: Alfred A. Knopf, 1997. Print. 104.

**Chapter 7. A Citizen of Cuba**

1. Jon Lee Anderson. *Che Guevara: A Revolutionary Life*. New York: Grove Press, 1997. Print. 390.

2. Daniel James. *Che Guevara: A Biography*. 1969. New York: Cooper Square Press, 2001. Print. 113.

3. Ernesto Che Guevara. *Reminiscences of the Cuban Revolutionary War*. Trans. Victoria Ortiz. New York: Monthly Review Press, 1968. Print. 258.

4. Jon Lee Anderson. *Che Guevara: A Revolutionary Life*. New York: Grove Press, 1997. Print. 453.

5. Che Guevara. *Guerrilla Warfare*. 1961. Lincoln, NE: University of Nebraska Press, 1998. Print. 7.

6. Jorge G. Castañeda. *Compañero: The Life and Death of Che Guevara*. Trans. Marina Castañeda. New York: Alfred A. Knopf, 1997. Print. 231.

**Chapter 8. Failure in Africa**

1. Jon Lee Anderson. *Che Guevara: A Revolutionary Life*. New York: Grove Press, 1997. Print. 535.

2. Daniel James. *Che Guevara: A Biography*. 1969. New York: Cooper Square Press, 2001. Print. 153.

3. Ernesto Che Guevara. *The African Dream: The Diaries of the Revolutionary War in the Congo*. Trans. Patrick Camiller. New York: Grove Press, 2000. Print. 24.

4. Ibid. 216.

5. Ibid. 182.

**Chapter 9. Ultimate Defeat**

1. Felix I. Rodriguez and John Weisman. *Shadow Warrior: The CIA Hero of a Hundred Unknown Battles*. New York: Simon and Schuster, 1989. Print. 169.

2. Jon Lee Anderson. *Che Guevara: A Revolutionary Life*. New York: Grove Press, 1997. Print. 634.

3. Ernesto Che Guevara. *The Diary of Che in Bolivia*. Calcutta, India: National Book Agency, 1968. Print. 170–171.

4. Jon Lee Anderson. *Che Guevara: A Revolutionary Life*. New York: Grove Press, 1997. Print. 733.

5. Fidel Castro. *Che: A Memoir by Fidel Castro*. 2nd ed. Ed. David Deutschmann. New York: Ocean Press, 2006. Print. 222.

6. Ernesto Che Guevara. *Venceremos! The Speeches and Writings of Ernesto Che Guevara*. Ed. John Gerassi. New York: Macmillan, 1968. Print. 424.

# INDEX

*African Dream, The,* 12
Arbenz, Jacobo, 47

*Back on the Road,* 12
Batista, Fulgencio, 7, 10, 44,
  45, 49, 53, 54, 61, 65, 66,
  67
Bayo, Alberto, 50
Bolivia, 12, 27, 43, 85–93
  base camp in Ñancahuazú
    region, 86–88
  battles, 87–92
  capture of Che Guevara,
    89–92
  revolution, 43, 85–93
*Bolivian Diary of Ernesto Che Guevara,
The,* 12

Castro, Fidel, 7, 11, 44, 45, 48,
  49–50, 52–55, 57–50, 64,
  66, 69, 74, 77, 78, 81, 82,
  85, 93
Castro, Raúl, 48, 54
Central Intelligence Agency,
  US, 46
Cienfuegos, Camilo, 11
Cienfuegos, Osmany, 79
Communism, 7, 12, 43, 44,
  45, 46, 47, 48, 58, 60, 66,
  70, 72, 77, 79, 86
Congo, 12, 76, 77–82
  coup, 81
  Dar es Salaam, Tanzania, 77,
    84
  Kabila, Laurent, 76, 78, 81
  Lake Tanganyika, 77, 78

Córdoba, Argentina, 17, 19,
  20, 22, 24, 26, 27, 29
Cuban army, 7, 8–11, 53, 54,
  57–60, 66
Cuban Missile Crisis, 72, 75
Cuban policies, 69, 71
Cuban Revolution,
  Battle of Alegría de Pío, 53,
    54
  Battle of El Bueycito, 58
  Battle of El Hombrito, 58, 59
  Battle of La Plata, 55
  Battle of Pino del Agua, 59
  Battle of Santa Clara, 7–10,
    54, 62
  march to Las Villas province,
    60–61
  rebel camps, 50, 59, 62
  revolutionary army, 6, 7, 9,
    11, 54, 55, 57, 58, 59, 62,
    67

*El Cubano Libre,* 59
Engels, Friedrich, 45, 47

Ferreyra, María del Carmen
  (Chichina), 29–30, 33, 34

Gadea, Hilda (wife), 45, 48,
  49, 54, 60, 65, 75
Granado, Alberto, 21, 27, 33,
  39, 42
*Granma,* 52–53
Guatemala City, Guatemala,
  45, 47
guerilla training, 49, 50, 59,
  75, 79, 81, 87

*Guerilla Warfare,* 12
Guevara, Ernesto,
  ancestry, 20
  asthma, 15–16, 17, 19, 21, 25,
    36, 56, 67, 78, 79, 89, 90
  capture, 89–92
  childhood, 14–22
  children, 49, 65, 68, 71, 75,
    91
  death, 92–93
  disguise, 77, 85, 86
  education, 18–22, 24–30,
    39–40
  marriages, 49, 60, 68
  military career, 50, 58,
    64–77
  nicknames, 15, 21, 45, 77
  travels, 26–28, 30, 32–40,
    42–44

Havana, Cuba, 8, 10, 11, 12,
  44, 62, 90, 91

imperialism, 43, 44, 76, 94
Instituto Nacional de Reforma
  Agraria, 69

Kennedy, John F., 72
Korda, Alberto, 10

La Cabaña, 11, 64–66,
*La Prensa,* 54
leftist governments, 43, 44
Lenin, Vladimir, 45, 46, 47
leprosariums, 27, 35, 36,
  38–39

Lynch, Ernesto Guevara
  (father), 14, 15, 16, 19, 20,
  21, 25, 54, 65

Machu Picchu, 36, 43
*Manifesto of the Communist Party,* 47
March, Aleida (wife), 60, 62,
  64, 68
Marx, Karl, 45, 47
Marxism, 46
Mexico City, Mexico, 47, 49,
  54
Misiones, Argentina, 15, 17
Molotov cocktails, 9, 50
*Motorcycle Diaries, The,* 12, 93

National Bank of Cuba, 69
*New York Times,* 66

Perón, Juan, 25, 26

Santa Clara University, 7
Serna, Celia de la (mother), 14,
  17, 18–20, 25, 38, 79
Sierra Maestra Mountains, 53,
  54, 55, 59
Soviet Union, 70, 72, 77

*Tackle,* 26
trade embargo, US, 71–72
26th of July Movement, 44, 45,
  53

United Nations General
  Assembly, 75

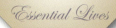
## ABOUT THE AUTHOR

Valerie Bodden is a freelance author and editor. She has written more than 100 children's nonfiction books. Her books have received positive reviews from *School Library Journal, Booklist, Children's Literature, ForeWord Magazine, Horn Book Guide, VOYA,* and *Library Media Connection.* Bodden lives in Wisconsin with her husband and their three children.

## PHOTO CREDITS

Time & Life Pictures/Getty Images, cover, 3, 13; Keystone/Getty Images, 6; Francoise De Mulder/Getty Images, 11; Apic/Getty Images, 14, 23, 41, 96; Bettmann/Corbis, 18, 42; AP Images, 24, 51, 64, 68, 73, 76, 84, 86, 99 (top), 99 (bottom); Canadian Press/AP Images, 27; Focus Features/Photofest, 31, 32, 97 (top); Red Line Editorial, Inc., 37; Library of Congress, 46; Harold Valentine/AP Images, 52, 61, 97 (bottom); Andrew St. George/AP Images, 56; Keystone/Stringer/Getty Images, 63; Tony Ortega/AP Images, 74; AFP/Getty Images, 83, 98; Jose Goitia/AP Images, 95